HOW Anime and Cartoons ARE MADE

by Noah Leatherland

Minneapolis, Minnesota

Credits
Images are courtesy of Shutterstock.com, unless otherwise stated.
Cover & Recurring – Pixel-Shot, MarbellaStudio, my.ordinarty, Natalia Ustyuzhantseva, Dooder, Rolau Elena, Natasha Pankina. 4–5 – Cast Of Thousands, tanaonte/Adobe Stock Images. 6–7 – Lightkite, WinWin artlab, LightField Studios. 8–9 – fizkes, Oliver Hoffmann. 10–11 – Muhammad Anuar bin Jamal, ONYXprj. 12–13 – fizkes, megaflopp. 14–15 – Frame Stock Footage, aijiro. 16–17 – Tutatamafilm. 18–19 – MadPixel, ESB Professional. 20–21 – bacterykey, Andrey_Popov. 22–23 – MarbellaStudio, Anait. 24–25 – Net Vector, Anait. 26–27 – DC Studio, PrinceOfLove. 28–29 –Leszek Glasner, Hispanolistic/iStock. 30–31 – PeopleImages.com - Yuri A.

Bearport Publishing Company Product Development Team
Publisher: Jen Jenson; Director of Product Development: Spencer Brinker; Editorial Director: Allison Juda; Editor: Cole Nelson; Editor: Tiana Tran; Production Editor: Naomi Reich; Art Director: Kim Jones; Designer: Kayla Eggert; Designer: Steve Scheluchin; Production Specialist: Owen Hamlin

Library of Congress Cataloging-in-Publication Data is available at www.loc.gov or upon request from the publisher.

ISBN: 979-8-89577-083-2 (hardcover)
ISBN: 979-8-89577-473-1 (paperback)
ISBN: 979-8-89577-200-3 (ebook

© 2026 BookLife Publishing
This edition is published by arrangement with BookLife Publishing.

North American adaptations © 2026 Bearport Publishing Company. All rights reserved. No part of this publication may be reproduced in whole or in part, stored in any retrieval system, or transmitted in any form or by any means, electronic, mechanical, photocopying, recording, or otherwise, without written permission from the publisher. Bearport Publishing is a division of FlutterBee Education Group.

For more information, write to Bearport Publishing, 3500 American Blvd W, Suite 150, Bloomington, MN 55431.

Contents

How Things Are Made 4

Cartoons vs. Anime 6

Ideas and Imagination 8

Character Design 10

Script Writing 12

Voice Acting 14

Storyboards 16

Animatics 18

Backgrounds 20

Final Art 22

Animation 24

Sound and Music 26

Release 28

Your Next Project 30

Glossary 31

Index 32

Read More 32

Learn More Online 32

How Things Are Made

Are you a creative person?

Your favorite books, movies, TV shows, and video games came from the minds of people just like you! It takes a group of talented makers to take these forms of entertainment from concept to creation.

Cartoons and anime are stories told with **animation**. Some are full movies. Others are TV shows split into shorter **episodes**.

There are many steps to creating these forms of entertainment. How are cartoons and anime made?

Cartoons vs. Anime

Cartoons and anime have slightly different art styles. Many cartoon characters are not very lifelike. They may look silly.

On the other hand, anime is more realistic. Its characters often have big eyes and colorful hair.

Although they may look a little different, cartoons and anime are made in the same way.

Anime originally came from Japan, but it is popular all over the world.

Ideas and Imagination

The first step to creating a cartoon or anime is coming up with an idea.

An idea might come from one creator working alone. Or a team of artists, writers, and **animators** might all help.

Cartoons and anime tell all kinds of stories. They can be about normal people or be tales that are more magical.

If something can be drawn, it can be turned into a cartoon or anime!

Character Design

An important early part of making a cartoon or anime is **designing** the characters. Each character needs to look different. This makes it easy for viewers to follow the story.

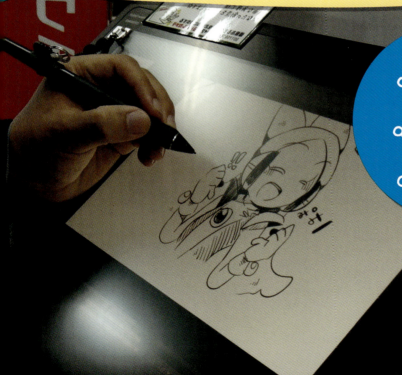

Some artists design characters digitally with tablets or computers.

10

These characters will have to be drawn many times. The artists need to think about how the characters will look doing different things.

Script Writing

To capture the story, cartoon and anime writers will make a script. They break down their story into different **scenes**.

Scripts say what the characters will do and say. They also describe where the characters are in their world.

After the script is finished, the writers read through it again. They may add or change scenes to make the story better.

Making changes to a script is called editing.

Voice Acting

Voice actors perform the **dialogue** for cartoons and anime.

Often, they start with table reads. All of the voice actors come together to read the script. This helps the actors know how to say their lines.

Then, it is time to record the dialogue. Sometimes, the actors do this together in the same room. Other times, they do it alone.

Some voice actors might record lines for many characters in the same cartoon or anime.

Storyboards

Artists make storyboards to plan how the cartoon or anime will look.

Storyboards are usually quick, black-and-white sketches of the scenes. The art is not very detailed. It is just the idea for scenes.

This step helps the artists and animators imagine how characters will look.

The artists can then work together to make changes until the storyboard looks just right.

A storyboard

Animatics

An animatic is a very early **version** of a cartoon.

Animatics are made from the storyboard drawings. The drawings are put together with spoken lines recorded by the voice actors.

Cartoons have only a short amount of time for each movie or episode. Animatics help the creators make sure their story will fit in that time.

Often, teams of artists make and watch animatics together to make sure everything looks right.

Backgrounds

Cartoons and anime use a lot of background art. This helps people know where the characters are in a scene.

Background artists design this art to fit with the style of the cartoon or anime.

Different backgrounds are needed for every place that the characters go in a story.

Background artists might make a few backgrounds of the same place from different **angles**.

Final Art

Other artists work on making finished drawings of the characters. They also draw the props, or the objects that characters use.

Artists might also have to draw out the main moments of action. These are called key frames.

Key frames show the different steps of something happening.

If a character jumps, artists might draw the character about to jump. Then, they could draw the character in the air and landing back on the ground.

Key Frames

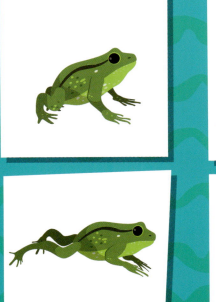

Animation

Animators connect the key frames. They make all the images that come between these moments.

When all of the art is put together, it looks like the image is moving.

A key frame

A key frame

A key frame

A key frame

Animators also make it look like the characters' mouths move when they speak. They match up the mouth movements with the voice actors' lines.

Lastly, the animated frames are put on top of the background art.

Sound and Music

There is more to hear in cartoons and anime than just dialogue. You might hear a character's footsteps or a huge explosion.

Sound designers make all these sounds and add them to the animation.

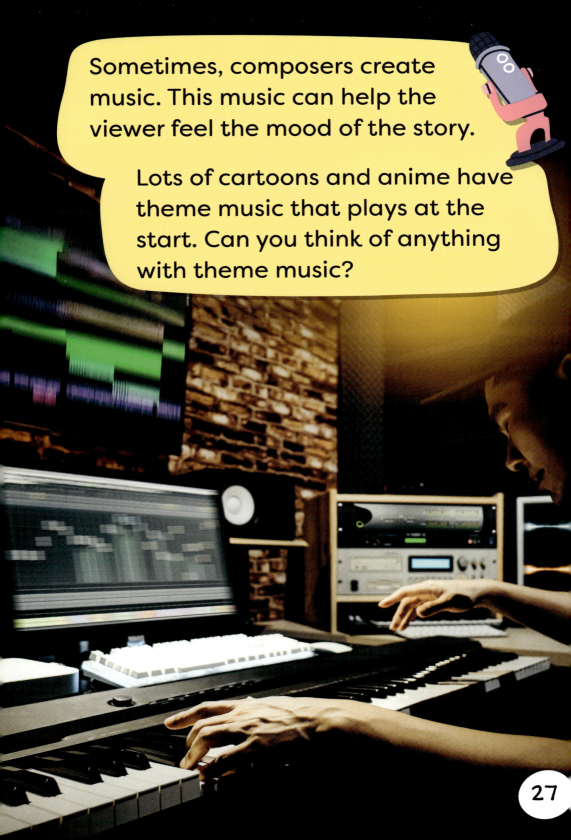

Sometimes, composers create music. This music can help the viewer feel the mood of the story.

Lots of cartoons and anime have theme music that plays at the start. Can you think of anything with theme music?

Release

Once the visuals and sounds are put together, cartoons and anime are ready to watch.

Some cartoons and anime are played on TV. Others can be watched online. A few are shown in movie theaters.

Anime usually comes from Japan. So, it is made in Japanese.

Before it goes to other countries, anime might be subbed. This means that **subtitles** are added. Some anime is dubbed. New dialogue is recorded in another language.

Sometimes, new voice actors record dubbed dialogue.

Your Next Project

Many people work together to create cartoons and anime. It takes a lot of teamwork.

What would you do to help create a cartoon or anime? The next big movie or TV show could be yours!

Glossary

animation a series of drawings that look like they are moving when seen one after another

animators artists who draw art to make it look like characters and objects in a cartoon or anime are moving

angles the different directions a character or background is seen on screen

designing deciding how something will look

dialogue words spoken between two or more characters

episodes shorter parts of a larger story

scenes sections of a story

subtitles words on the bottom of the screen that tell the viewer what is being said

version a form of a particular thing

Index

actors 14–15, 18, 25, 29
animators 8, 19, 24–25
episodes 5, 19
frames 22–25
props 22
sketches 16
subtitles 29
TV 4–5, 28, 30
writers 8, 12–13

Read More

Garbot, Dave. *Let's Draw Cartoon Characters (Let's Make Art).* Beverly, MA: Walter Foster Jr., 2023.

Leatherland, Noah. *How Comics and Manga Are Made (From Concept to Creation).* Minneapolis: Bearport Publishing Company, 2026.

Learn More Online

1. Go to **FactSurfer.com** or scan the QR code below.
2. Enter "**Anime and Cartoons**" into the search box.
3. Click on the cover of this book to see a list of websites.